What Child Is This?

A Christmas Songbook for Voice & Piano

T0056025

G. SCHIRMER, Inc.

DISTRIBUTED BY

HAL•LEONARD®
CORPORATION
7777 W. BLUEMOUND RD. P.O. BOX 13819 MILWAUKEE, WI 53213

ED. 3058

Contents

What Child is This

William C. Dix

"Greensleeves"
Old English Melody
Arranged by Ernst Victor Wolff

This, this is Christ the King, Whom shep - herds guard and an - gels sing:

Haste, haste to bring Him laud, The Babe, the Son of

Ma - ry. Why lies He in such

Hail, hail— the Word made flesh, The Babe, the Son— of Ma - ry!

So bring Him in - cense, gold and myrrh, Come,

peas - ant, King— to own Him, The King of kings sal - va - tion brings, Let

lov - ing hearts en - throne Him. Raise, raise the song on high; The

vir - gin sings her lull - a - by: Joy, joy, for Christ is born, The

Babe, the Son of Ma - ry!

I Wonder as I Wander

Collected by
John Jacob Niles

Appalachian Carol*
Adapted and arranged by John Jacob Niles
and Lewis Henry Horton

*In the version of John Jacob Niles, included in "Songs of the Hill Folk", published by G. Schirmer, Inc.

If Je - sus had want - ed for an - y wee thing, A star in the sky, or a bird on the wing, Or all of God's an - gels in heav'n for to sing, He sure - ly could have it, 'cause he was the King.

Joseph, Dearest Joseph

German Carol
English Version* by
Percy Dearmer (1867-1936)

Normand Lockwood

Andante ($\quad$ = 100)

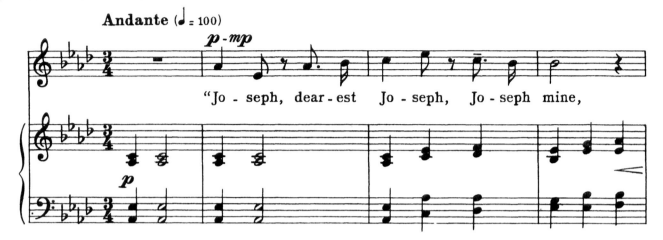

14

Cantique de Noël

Christmas Song

Edited by Carl Deis

Adolphe Adam

O ho - ly night!__ the stars are bright-ly
Mi - nuit,__ Chré - tien,__ c'est l'heu - re so - len-

shin - ing, It is the night of the dear Sav-iour's birth;
nel - le Où l'Hom-me-Dieu des-cen-dit jus-qu'à nous,

Long lay the
Pour ef - fa-

world__ in sin and er-ror pin - ing, Till he ap-peared, and the soul felt its worth.
cer__ la tache o - ri - gi-nel - le Et de son père ar - rê-ter le cour-roux.

A
Le

cresc.

thrill of hope the wea-ry world re-joic - es, For yon - der breaks a new and glo-rious morn.

mon- de en-tier tres - sail-le d'es - pé-ran - ce A cet - te nuit qui lui donne un sau - veur.

f

Fall_____ on your knees!_____ O hear_____ the an-gel voic - es! O

Peu - ple, à ge - noux!_____ at - tends_____ ta dé - li - vran - ce. No-

night_____ di - vine!_____ O night_____ when Christ was born!_____ O

ël! No - ël!_____ voi - ci_____ le Ré - demp-teur,_____ No-

cresc.

night_____ di - vine!_____ O night, O_____ night di - vine!

ël!_____ No - ël!_____ voi - ci le_____ Ré-demp-teur.

dim.

Led by the
De - no - tre

light___ of Faith se-rene-ly beam - ing, With glow-ing hearts, by His cra - dle we stand;
foi___ que la lu-miè-re-ar-den - te nous gui-de tous au ber-ceau de l'en-fant,

So, led by light of a star sweet-ly gleam - ing, Here came the wise men from___ the O - rient
com-me au-tre-fois une é-toi - le bril-lan - te y con-dui-sit les chefs___ de l'o - ri-

land. The King of Kings lay thus in low-ly man - ger, In all our tri - als
ent. Le Roi des Rois naît dans une hum-ble crè - che; puis-sants du jour, fiers

Sung by the Shepherds

from A Hymn of the Nativity
by Richard Crashaw

Music by Virgil Thomson
based on the *Pange Lingua*

Guild-ed in the Beams___ of Earth-ly Kings,___

Slip-p'ry souls___ in smil-ing Eyes,___ But to

poor Shep-herds, sim-ple things,_ That use no var-nish,

no oil'd Arts,__ But lift____ clean hands__

full of clear____ hearts.

Meno mosso

Yet when young A - pril's bride-groom show'rs Shall bless__ the fruit-ful Mai__

last, in fire of thy fair Eyes,___ We'll burn,___

our own best___ sac - - ri -

fice.___

Buffalo, March 1963

Come to the Stable with Jesus

Daniel S. Twohig

Geoffrey O' Hara

love Him and wor-ship Him there,_____ With Jo-seph and

Ma - ry, the Wise Men and Kings, In mu - sic our

hearts now can share._____ Come to the sta-ble and

gaze on the scene, The Christ Child, His beau - ty to

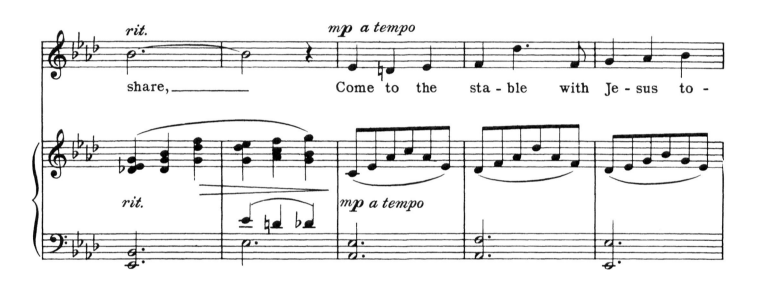

share,_____ Come to the sta - ble with Je - sus to -

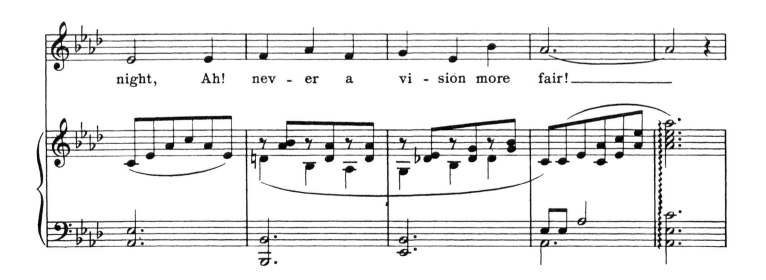

night, Ah! nev - er a vi - sion more fair!_____

Come to the sta - ble with Je - sus to - night, Where an - gels' glad songs fill the air; _____ We lift up our voic - es to

Sav - iour and King; Such mu - sic! there's none to com -

pare!_____ Come with the Wise Men who fol - lowed the

Star: The Shep-herds are kneel-ing in prayer._____

36

Come to the sta-ble with Je-sus to-night, Ah! nev-er a

vi - sion more fair!

And love Him and wor-ship Him there.

Christmas Candle

Kate Louise Brown

Elinor Remick Warren

dar - ling Christ-Child sweet.

He is com - ing in the snow, As he came so long a - go, When the

stars set o'er the hill; When the town is dark and still, He

comes, _____ He comes to do the Fa - - ther's

will. _____

espr.

mp

pp

mp

Lit - tle can - dle, spread thy ray, Make His path-way light as day;

espr.

poco cresc.

mp

poco cresc.

Let some door stand o - pen wide For this guest, this guest of

Christ-mas-tide, Dear-er than all,_____ than all else be-

side.____ Lit - tle Je - sus, come to me, Let my heart thy

The Christ-child Lives

Words by
Carrie P. Kittel

Music by
Muriel K. Davis

O Heav'n-ly star with radi-ant light Lead us a-gain this Christ-mas night. O Ho - ly Babe to Thee we bring our lives As hum-ble of-fer-ing, To Thee our King.

For Mrs. Carl Kaufmann

The First Christmas

Elizabeth Fleming

Celius Dougherty

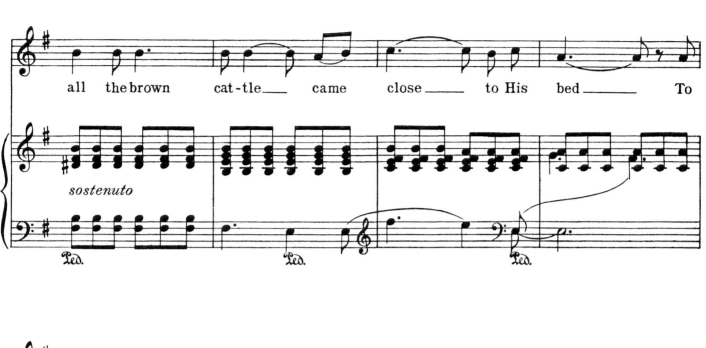

all the brown cat-tle___ came close___ to His bed___ To

see the wee___ Ba - by a - sleep in___ their shed,___ To

see the wee___ Ba - by a - sleep in their shed.___

Soft - ly sing, soft - ly sing, soft - ly

sing._____ His car - ols were

prais - es of love and good will_____ That rose___ in the

mid - night, so calm and _ so still, To her - ald the ear - li-est

Christ - mas we know, _____ When Je - sus was lit - tle, a

long while a - go, _____ When Je - sus was lit - tle, a

con pedale

long while a - go.

pp *ten.*

Soft - ly sing, soft - ly sing, soft - - ly

pp *colla voce*

sing.

For Thomas Michael Tolliver Niles on being five years of age

Jesus, Jesus, Rest Your Head

Adapted from the singing
of three people in Hardin County, Kentucky

Adapted by John Jacob Niles

Je - sus, Je - sus, rest your head, You has got a man - ger bed.

All the e - vil folk on earth Sleep in feath - ers at their birth.

Je - sus, Je - sus, rest your head, You has got a man - ger bed.

All the e - vil folk on earth Sleep in feath-ers at their birth.

Je - sus, Je - sus, rest your head, You has got a man - ger bed.

2. To that man - ger came then wise men, Bring-ing things from hin and yon.

For the moth - er and the fa - ther And the bless - ed lit - tle Son.

Christmas at the Cloisters

William Hoffman

John Corigliano

Jesus of Nazareth

Jésus de Nazareth

A. Porte
English words by Henry F. Chorley

Charles Gounod

Moderato quasi andante

Tho' poor be the cham - ber, come here, come and a - dore;_____
Né dans u - ne crê - che, di - vin Ré - demp - teur,_____

Lo! the Lord of Heav - en hath to mor-tals giv - en
i - ci-bas_ je prê - che, i - ci-bas_ je prê - che

life_ for - ev - er - more,
les_ ver-tus du cœur,

life for - ev - er - more,_____
les ver-tus du cœur,_____

life for - ev - er - more._____
les_ ver-tus du cœur._____

Shep - herds who fold - ed your flocks be - side you,
N'é - touf - fez plus la voix des saints o - ra - cles;

Tell what was told by an - gel voic - es near:_____ To
pes - ti - fé - rés, lé - preux du la - za - reth,_____ Es-

life__ for - ev - er - more.__
*les__ ver-tus du cœur.*__

Kings from a far land, draw near and__ be-
Plein de pi - tié pour la fem - me a - dul-

hold Him, Led by the beam whose warn - ing bade ye
tè - re qui s'a - ge - nouil - le et pleu - re en mon che-

come;_____ Your crowns cast down,_____ with
min,_____ Je dis à ceux qui lui

robe roy - al en - fold Him; Your King de -
jet - tent la pier - - re, sur vo - tre

scends to earth from bright - er home._____
*cœur a - - vez - vous mis la main?*____

Tho' poor be the cham - ber, come here, come and a - dore;____
*Né dans u - ne crê - che, di - vin Ré - demp - teur,*____

Lo! the Lord of Heav - en hath to mor-tals giv - en
i - ci-bas_ je prê - che, i - ci-bas_ je prê - che

life_ for - ev er - more._____
les_ ver - tus du cœur._____

Wind, to the ce - dars pro -
A - veu - gles nés,_____ mu -

claim the joy - ful sto - ry; Wave of the
ets, pa - ra - ly - ti - ques, pau - vres per -

sea,_____ the ti - dings bear a - far._____ The
dus, boi - teux, sourds ap - pro - chez._____ Du

dore;_____ Lo! the Lord of Heav - en
teur,_____ i - ci - bas je prê - che,

hath to mor - tals giv - en life_ for - ev - er -
i - ci - bas_ je prê - che les_ ver - tus du

more, life for - ev - er - more,_____
cœur, les ver - tus du cœur,_____

life_ for - ev - er - more._____
les_ ver - tus du cœur._____

Mary's Soliloquy
from the cantata:
"The St. Luke Christmas Story"

Lucy Vessey

Cecil Effinger

Mar - y heard the An - gels sing: "There shall be a lit - tle King

born to you, And He shall be— Great - er than all roy - al - ty."

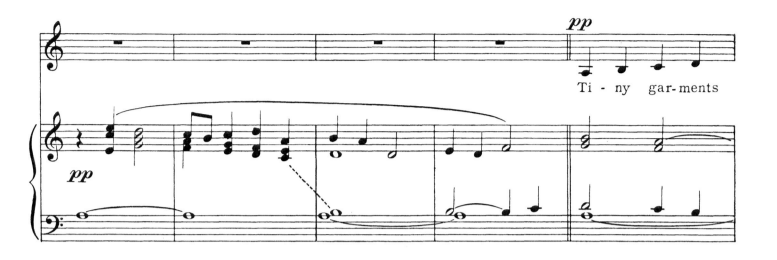

Ti - ny gar-ments

fine - ly sewn As she kept her vig - il lone,__ Mar - y smil'd, Her

Child would be__ Strong and brave as man should be! Fears and doubts were

The Star of Bethlehem

F.E. Weatherly

Stephen Adams

72

a tempo.
From
f
dim.
Ped.
quasi parlando.
street to street it led me, by many a man-sion fair, It shone thro' din-gy casement on
p
many a gar-ret bare; From highway on to highway, thro' alleys dark and cold, And
rall.
a tempo.
where it shone the darkness was flooded all with gold. Sad hearts for-got their sor - row, Rough
p

yond the waste of ruin - ed lives, the press of hu - man

things; A - bove the toil and shad - ow, A -

bove the want and woe, My old self and it's

dark - ness seem'd left on earth be - low. And

There's a Song in the Air

Christmas Song

J. G. Holland*

Oley Speaks

Andantino semplice

Allegretto con moto

There's a song___ in the air, There's a star___ in the sky, There's a moth - er's deep pray'r, And a ba - by's low cry;___ And the star___ rains its fire___ While the Beau - ti - ful sing, For the

man-ger of Beth-le-hem cra - dles a King.___There's a tu' - mult of

joy___ O'er the won - der-ful birth,___ For the Vir - gin's sweet

boy___ Is the Lord of_ the earth. And the star__rains its fire While the

Beau - ti-ful sing, For the man - ger of Beth-le-hem__ cra - dles a

Noël, Noël, Bells are Ringing

Alice Grainger[*]

Wilbur Chenoweth

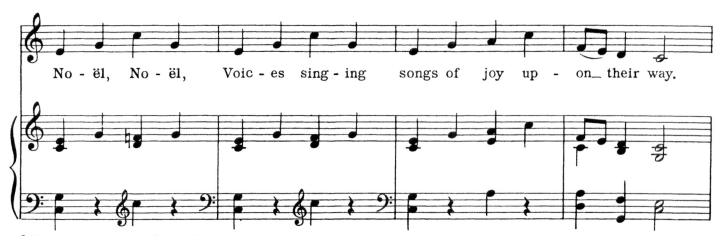

*Words used by special permission.

Let the joy-ous car-ols ring, Praise to God, our Lord and King.

mp a tempo No - ël, No - ël, Bells are ring - ing, Peace on earth this Christ-mas day.

a tempo No - ël, No - ël, Bells are ring - ing

through the clear and frost-y air. No - ël, No - ël, Glad-ness bring-ing

To Mr. FRANCIS FISCHER POWERS.

The Birthday of a King

W.H. Neidlinger

sky was bright with a ho-ly light, O'er the place where Je-sus

lay:. Al - le - lu - ia! O how the an - gels sang, Al - le-

lu - ia! how it rang; And the

sky was bright with a ho - ly light, 'Twas the

birth-day of a King.

'Twas a hum - ble birth-place, but oh! how much God gave to us that day, From the man - ger bed, what a path has led What a

The Repose of the Holy Family
from "Childhood of Christ"

Hector Berlioz

Allegretto grazioso. M.M. ♩. = 52.

PIANO.

Tenor. THE NARRATOR.

So through the de - sert forth they went, Till be - hold, they

came _____ to a mea - - dow,

Where palm-trees o'er the herb-age bent, And o'er a

foun - tain in the sha - dow. Then said Jo - seph, "Let us a -

light, By this plea - sant well____ Of flow - ing wa - ter, Safe

from the eye of Slaugh - ter, Rest____ we to - night." The

Child he slum - ber - ed, And then Ma - ry, the Mo - ther, Light - ed a - down, and answering,

said, "Be - hold a sha - dy bower, Lo! the bed of li - ly flower, That the

pp   *poco f*   *dim.*   *p*

shades a-round were clos-ing, (Je-sus up-on his mo-ther's breast,) Did the

wea - - ry Three For a - while take their rest.

O'er whom, while now sweet-ly they sleep, Countless an-gels of

Heav'n round a-bout vi-gils keep, On their knees the In-fant a-dor-ing.

Al - le - lu - ja, Al - le - lu - ja!

What Songs Were Sung

Words and music by
John Jacob Niles

Tenderly ♩= c. 66 *(in a story-telling manner)*

We can-not tell, we do not know What stars shone down so long a-go, When Mar-y birthed her own sweet Son And peace and love be-came as one. The Son of God, as scrip-tures said, Was Vir-gin born in a ti-ny shed, Where sim-ple shep-herds

stood hard by While heav'n-ly sound filled up the sky.

Now let us stand, un-cov-ered all, Be-fore this crèche in___ low-ly stall, Where kings and an-gels dig-ni-fy God's_ gift, His Son, in hu-mil-i-ty.

We do not know, we can-not tell What

The Twelve Days of Christmas

Par-tridge in a Pear Tree. On the Third day of Christ-mas my

true love sent to me Three French Hens, Two Tur-tle Doves and a

Par-tridge in a Pear Tree. On the Fourth day of Christ-mas my

true love sent to me Four Call-ing Birds, Three French Hens,

Four Call-ing Birds, Three French Hens, Two Tur-tle Doves and a

Par-tridge in a Pear Tree. On the Ninth day of Christ-mas my

true love sent to me Nine La-dies danc-ing, Eight Maids a-milk-ing,

Seven Swans a-swimming, Six Geese a-lay-ing, Five Gold Rings,

Four Calling Birds, Three French Hens,   Two Turtle Doves and a Par-tridge in a Pear

Tree.   On the E - leventh day of Christ-mas my   true love sent to me

E-le-ven Pi-pers pi-ping, Ten Lords a - leap-ing, Nine   La-dies danc-ing,

poco marcato

Eight Maids a - milk-ing, Seven Swans a - swim-ming, Six Geese a - lay-ing,